Loose Bricks

Loose Bricks
Copyright © 2025 BOSTON GORDON

All rights reserved. No part of this publication may be reproduced or transmitted in any form or by any means without the prior written permission of the publisher, except for brief excerpts for the purpose of criticism and review.

For permissions and information on ordering books, contact operations@smallharborpublishing.com.

Cover art: Cyrus Finegan, "Loose Bricks"
Interior design: Eliza Carlson
Editor: Eliza Carlson
Publisher: Allison Blevins
Director: Kristiane Weeks-Rogers

LOOSE BRICKS
BOSTON GORDON
ISBN 978-1-957248-52-3
Harbor Editions,
an imprint of Small Harbor Publishing

Loose Bricks

Boston Gordon

Harbor Editions
Small Harbor Publishing

For James, Ernie, and Frankie—my outer worlds.

"Texting is a supremely secretive medium of communication—it's like passing a note—and this means we should be very careful what we use it for."

—Lynne Truss

"The poem is a form of texting . . . it's the original text. It's a perfecting of a feeling in language—it's a way of saying more with less, just as texting is."

—Carol Ann Duffy

July 6, 2012

so many songs at Frank's tonight

ruined my life

> "Ex-Factor"
>
> "In My Life"
>
> "Daydream Believer"
>
> "Me and Bobby McGee"
>
> "Love on Top"
>
> "Wagon Wheel"
>
> "In the Aeroplane Over the Sea"

kamikaze shots and high life ponies

every song more preposterous

threw a dart so hard I missed everything relevant

hit the floor

July 7, 2012

Jhett from Tabu last night
meet at 43rd and Baltimore
Green Line Café

July 12, 2012

bottle rockets go off on Girard Street roll the window up in JK's car

bad luck song comes on the radio all the times you accused me

checking out some person's ass or face

or smile or curled lip

July 22, 2012

Wild raspberries

      river loam

feet stuck in the brambles

      your bare ass in my hands

even thinking of *these* things

      I do not miss you

July 26, 2012

red hair makes me feel unwell

August 7, 2012

couldn't sleep

      thinking about

      no condom

biked to the harbor

      at dawn

      only harbor seals

then the pharmacy

      at the open

      pregnancy test on sale

two for $6.99

September 12, 2012

After we fucked, their friends walked by
and kept saying *oh you're that Boston, you're that Boston.*
Late and drunk and far from home.
A cab slowed down and waved for me to get in
I shook my head, kept strutting, and thought, no I'll walk.
I'm Boston, I'm Boston.

September 27, 2012

Iowa is a thousand miles closer than Idaho.

And you were right about the end, it didn't make a difference.

October 2, 2012

Is there anything more slick than wet red brick?

November 27, 2012

I met a boy

I couldn't get off

my mind.

January 7, 2013

To be counted

        fever dreams

again

January 8, 2013

Harvard Square:

I slug a lager
        field the soft gestures of a girl who

      thinks she likes me.

January 11, 2013

Footprints in the snow.

A kid harasses me in the parking lot.

So cold outside

      his spit on my neck

                              freezes

February 11, 2013

Guffaw.

February 18, 2013

Fuck it.

I can't

      write a poem.

I can't

      be the cowboy

I'm not the cowboy

      or his boot

            or the scuff marks

                  on the toe of his brown leather boot.

February 20, 2013

I'm not the marvelous cowboy I dreamed I'd be.
I'm not even his boot, not even a scuff mark
at the toe of his brown leather boot.

It's all rug burn, rough
on my skin like the voices I can still hear,
bellow *"fuck yourself and die you fucking fag"*
as I'm knocked onto hot macadam.

I spat in his face. I wanted to feel brave.

There were the dicks who poured Kool-Aid onto my shoes
and hocked foamy saliva on the back of my head.

There were ones who jerked off on the body of my car,
jizz in crosses on the hood.

There were the busted knees
of my jeans.

March 3, 2013

J got angry with me for chewing too loudly, and I'm pissed that my first thought was to starve to death.

March 22, 2013

When I first got sick, they held me while I cried. Later, shook my shoulders and asked

> *what the fuck is wrong with you?*

March 31, 2013

I buy a different tea

for every one

of their unpredictable moods.

June 30, 2013

A nightmare: I finally get off the train in Philadelphia, but Philadelphia isn't there, and I have to find J. Hanna, who always wears a bowtie, finds me and walks me to J's grandparents' house on the bay side of the town. I see no one I know, except J's cousin, who hugs me softly while she cries. Suddenly, I have to go, to run away. I have a full blown panic attack in my dream. I run and tell Hanna I need to get on the train to Philly, that we must be getting close, given how far I've run. When we get on the train I see Cate who tells me we're in Baltimore. How did I miss Philly? I can't understand it.

July 2, 2013

I am the hidden parts in a machine.

August 8, 2013

Hi

September 6, 2013

What bliss to hear a freight train in bed at night

in that old miserable apartment

where I don't miss you.

September 7, 2013

I'm waiting

      to see

when I finally

          close the door

               on you.

October 6, 2013

Despite ourselves.

October 18, 2013

Loving is like

being alone.

October 27, 2013

J shrugs me off again.

Time to sing *so long*.

November 2, 2013

Why are storms named after people?
Will you always feel like a storm to me?

November 24, 2013

Please
        fuck me
                like the Song of Songs.
                      I just need to be touched
                              by someone.
                                      Anyone.

November 30, 2013

I used to measure my life in train rides to visit and come. Now I measure my life in days since I've had sex. Like a sign in a factory. Like a terrible accident. 44 days since anyone has wanted me. 82 days since anyone's made me come.

December 1, 2013

There's this moment in my dreams when I find the nearest man in the bar, grab him into the bathroom by his collar, and give him a single sticky kiss on the neck before I pinch my fingers, unbuttoning his Levi's, and jerk him off until I feel as dirty and as sorry as I do when J tells me to leave them alone. In the dreams, I'm always a man,

>but that's not the point.

December 30, 2013

Are you ever in the bar and you feel a guy's cock on your hip and you know it's because today you look like a queer trick and you consider it even without the money because to be fucked for the sake of it is to be wanted

>like meat in your teeth?

Jan 2, 2014

One red thread.

> Like that hair again.

> Oh god.

Jan 10, 2014

Write about darts. Or the fight in the bar on your birthday. The man who punched you on the cheek when you told him to fuck off and stop grabbing your partner's ass. The darts you and Matt threw to blow off the violence. Like boys bonded together. The way you bonded over everything this year.

Jan 14, 2014

I have not told my garden yet.

Jan 16, 2014

1400 block of Spruce Street, across from the Kimmel Center, Biron.

> Licensed Clinical Social Worker
> Panic Disorder

Jan 21, 2014

I grew up in a brittle town with a soul like hot macadam

Jan 27, 2014

It began with a whistle.

February 2, 2014

That was the first day I knew I was a man. I was a redwing blackbird caught in the wire outside town hall.

February 5, 2014

I'm obsessed with the histories of the people I crush on.

February 14, 2014

Come bite my neck on Fabric Row.

February 17, 2014

Overheard: *"I like my porn like I like my rodeo. Bull riding and bareback."*

February 13, 2014

J in May. My body is in a lurch. They nip at my breasts, and I'm grateful and mended like bones. Thank you for the time to take care of my body. It takes up too much space. It doesn't deserve even this.

February 25, 2014

Whiskeying. Again.

February 26, 2014

You know the way guys spit on each other in pornos? Yeah, I feel like that tonight.

March 6, 2014

Whiskey John

March 17, 2014

teeth in jars

March 24, 2014

bobcat yawn

April 26, 2014

The lament of the attached queer.

May 1, 2014

Make a dinner date with M and D to discuss polyamory.

May 9, 2014

Happy Birthday

to

me.

May 14, 2014

A dream: the tow truck breaks down

and I'm kissing James again, and they tell me

    I won this time

and it was a mistake

    for J to trust them.

May 15, 2014

"You can't help me now."

June 14, 2014

Hilton Garden, Room 764, trans health conference play party.

June 18, 2014

Loose bricks, crow planet.

June 13, 2014

The anxiety, the cure, the quiet place.

June 23, 2014

blunder

June 25, 2014

quiet as a broken jaw

June 26, 2014

If you just ask for there to be a fire pit it will be there and be okay.

July 3, 2014

A note to J for when they are sober: When I said I wanted to talk about this when you were sober you said I was undermining you. You said you were jealous James and I got a hotel and you didn't think that was fair. You demanded to know why I wouldn't just be okay with {redacted} coming to our house and sleeping in our bed. You told me I only pay attention to you for fourteen seconds and then I just ignore you. You said you didn't feel like I loved you. You made a lot of comments about having sex with {redacted} in a very forward way that after some time made me feel uncomfortable.

July 6, 2014

The end to the treatise of not fucking.

July 20, 2014

The bird decides not to eat out of your hand. Chain bikes up to parking meters, wish suddenly and hard for something, card games.

July 24, 2014

free porn name: Flasher Gordon

July 27, 2014

The death of a train car is slow.

July 29, 2014

They are still drunk at 10 a.m., head down on the table, drinking club soda at the South Street Diner, talking about how they're not bitter about {redacted} breaking up with them: "I don't care, look how great I'm doing!"

July 30, 2014

Missed my bus stop cause I don't know James' streets—the deliciousness of new love.

August 8, 2014

Crazy for them,
       I cross the river
where I first loved them
         on my way to Sarah's house
for filler sex.
       I think about them
and nothing else.
       I think about the people
they loved
       before me
and ache with dread.

August 11, 2014

Someone hit me over the head.

Hard.

Was it them?

I think it was right after my birthday.

We were all supposed to go fishing that day.

I ripped my sleeves off because the way my head was swollen made my arms feel tied to cannonballs.

We had wrestled?

Or had I ducked into a cab too fast and too stoned for depth perception?

Something split my skull that night.

I think they pinned me on the bed and punched me in the jaw and my ears rang

       like being haunted.

I was the sculpture.

They made me a sculpture?

They threw me against it.

They were so important.

August 18, 2014

Write about the stores on Fabric Row. The shears. The fabric torn apart. Write about you torn apart.

August 19, 2014

The thing where James kisses their hand and then touches the car roof while going through a yellow light. *For luck.*

August 21, 2014

Biting into tomatoes like they're sweet peaches.

August 25, 2014

Dreamt Link and James were getting married, and *I was the best man.* We wore dark red suits, and they had dark red rings. I was so happy for them and so miserable at the same time.

After it was over, we were in the other room and I said it's easier now than later.

And James said

I know

and dropped down on one knee.

I was wearing their Boy George hat.

September 6, 2014

Matching bites from fire ants—blood brothers.

September 8, 2014

lousy at poker

September 16, 2014

They put an arcade in an old garage. I bought a drink. I kissed some man happy birthday. I waited by the jukebox for them. I knew they weren't coming. Just when the jukebox got too loud, and my head started to hurt, there they were.

I still can't believe they came.

September 28, 2014

American White Oak.

       A fire on 4th Street.

October 1, 2014

On May 1st, I did not think I would love them.

October 11, 2014

How can I trust anyone?

October 14, 2014

J took the mattress when they moved out. Steve the Navy vet, sells me a cheap one under the 25th Street train overpass. I kind of wanted to give him a handjob cause he sold me such a cheap mattress and asked for basically nothing in return. His back hurts, and he can't work over the table, or he'll lose his disability. He helped me carry it up to the 5th floor. I wanted to thank him, to let me give him something more. Maybe it was what I needed.

November 1, 2014

gestures

November 2, 2014

Remind James to drop off their rent check tomorrow.

November 14, 2014

Songs I heard last night that felt like an old dream:

> "Antichrist Television Blues"
>
> "The Purple Bottle"
>
> "Dark of the Matinee"
>
> "Dreamboat"
>
> "Use It"
>
> "The Bleeding Heart Show"
>
> "Dress Up in You"

I can hardly remember how it was before.

November 25, 2014

900 days since she cut you loose.

                                                Independence Day.

December 2, 2014

This is the worst fucking mattress I've ever slept on.

December 17, 2014

Romantic notion:
to ride
on the back
of a bike
on pegs.

December 31, 2014

My cover band must perform "See You Again" by Miley Cyrus.

January 7, 2015

I remember the first time someone called me Boston.

January 16, 2015

The feeling when you stick your face in the freezer in summer.

January 22, 2015

Write a poem called "General Delivery."

January 31, 2015

Overheard: *"Was I on drugs or just very manic?"*

February 19, 2015

$9.25 for smokes

    $10.00 pitcher of lager

        $3.60 for subway tokens

            a full day

February 26, 2015

Death card poem: Well, I *am*

 always

    shedding

        my skin.

March 22, 2015

We've been cooped up. When we make it to the gas station, it's lollipops and chewing tobacco and gas leaks into greasy puddles on the concrete.

March 26, 2015

Young boys in old bodies. Old boys in young bodies.

March 28, 2015

160 pounds

April 2, 2015

Motion sickness is your brain thinking you've been poisoned.

April 20, 2015

I am never a hero in my own dreams.

May 19, 2015

paper ships paper ghosts piano strings

May 20, 2015

"Now I just sleep beneath your floor."

May 27, 2015

Hiccuping is vestigial from when we were frogs.

May 30, 2015

What is the word for fear of blushing?

June 1, 2015

June

June 3, 2015

jackdaws

June 24, 2015

The trope of alcoholic fathers is so prevalent

you barely flinch

when mine pulls out his dick

                              and pisses on your beloved old car.

June 28, 2015

Overheard: *"Dave Matthews songs are sometimes kind of creepy. You just get the feeling that he wants to eat women."*

June 30, 2015

erythrophobia

July 20, 2015

Write something about when you did that miserable couples therapy with J.

July 29, 2015

When I finally found them,

        they were crying about their ex-boyfriend

on the couch in their underwear

        with a bowl of ramen

ready to catch their bawling

        and steam up their glasses.

August 12, 2015

peaches and cash

August 22, 2015

A Buddhist monk plays scratch-offs in this gas station. I will wonder about this forever.

September 15, 2015

Overheard: *"What Mister Rogers hell is this?"*

September 24, 2015

Overheard: *"I had sex with a married man on Yom Kippur."*

October 18, 2015

Don't forget to say *oh*.

October 23, 2015

I fell in love

        on Juniper Street,

                on Quince Street,

                        on Chancellor Street.

In the alleyways. Boys touching each other.

October 25, 2015

genetically cannot smell skunks

November 6, 2015

It was late enough I could smoke in the subway station undisturbed.

November 8, 2015

I had a dream about this room once.

November 11, 2015

Write about dress codes. About your deep fear of being forced to wear a skirt as a child.

November 12, 2015

That guy who carves soapstone figures on 2nd and Market gave me one of his creations. When I lose it, I'll wonder forever. How careless I can be with things that mean so much to other people.

November 23, 2015

Overhead talking about football: *"You play one overdramatic game of fetch, and suddenly you're popular."*

November 25, 2015

selective anosmia

December 2, 2015

I think the biggest fish in the tank at Nick's Bar died.

December 9, 2015

Why does Coca-Cola taste like blood?

December 10, 2015

Everyone in this Wawa is either a nurse or a cop, but I'm just sad

and wondering

where I can find

James.

December 13, 2015

That's how you keep things you can't keep.

December 21, 2015

Imagine you're on a mountain.

Your dad is drunk in the basement,

but you're on the mountain.

December 31, 2015

roses blooming on New Year's Eve outside Christ Church

January 12, 2016

They tell me how much they worry about my cruising.

January 19, 2016

Write about crows atop cords of lumber.

February 7, 2016

"I wish we had forties" —James

March 23, 2016

I'm tired of thinking about my body.

I'm tired of thinking about my father in the basement.

April 15, 2016

Flying Biscuits for breakfast in Atlanta

May 26, 2016

Remember the first time

they asked me to wear my boots

for them.

They love leather

and my butch cleavage.

June 7, 2016

I'll change my government name just in time to suck dick for health insurance.

July 2, 2016

Who the hell was I fucking on Market Street when the fireworks went off?

July 20, 2016

Raised $293 for the Orlando fund.

July 27, 2016

A boy I know dies too young.

August 3, 2016

Imagine this. Two boys in the rail yard,

two boys in a boxcar playing roulette

with a deck of tarot cards and a strobe light.

August 4, 2016

like pollen

August 7, 2016

They used to throw Molotov cocktails at their old high school.

I think *oh my god you would have been the teenage anarchist of my dreams.*

August 16, 2016

Too hot to take a piss anyway.

August 22, 2016

I never write about snow because I'm in love with a blooming tree.

August 27, 2016

Jacob.

August 29, 2016

Monday ad sales blues. Do you know what it feels like to be a landline? In this decade?

September 24, 2016

Long ago a man taught me there was more to be afraid of than thunderstorms.

September 26, 2016

I swear I can feel my anxiety in my ass.

October 10, 2016

Christian and Passyunk. Took pictures for insurance.

November 16, 2016

Buy James a magnifying glass to look at my dick with.

December 1, 2016

The moment I lose my job again.

December 5, 2016

Chapter 21

December 18, 2016

Being a slut saved my life.

December 29, 2016

cicadas

December 30, 2016

I want to talk about

spit.

February 8, 2017

Been unemployed more than employed this year.

What makes a bad job?

February 10, 2017

A total void instead of anxiety.

February 11, 2017

Anxiety as a sweet but skittish animal that lives inside of me.

February 27, 2017

Bring kombucha and creamer to the hotel for James.

March 22, 2017

California.

The trees

        drained

                their rainy loads

                        on me.

April 1, 2017

There was this afternoon

I drove through the woods

and I couldn't stop thinking about them

even though all they were to me then was a

tongue.

April 24, 2017

I am the captain of my own cunt.

May 19, 2017

Oh, but what is it like to bury your nose in a boy with breasts?

June 7, 2017

Breaking one's wrist is cumbersome.

June 15, 2017

St. Augustine meditated for hours to control his erection, and I repay him by grabbing any hard cock that wants me.

June 21, 2017

lucky boon

July 19, 2017

Use the word bluffs in a poem

to mean both cliffs
        and bluffing
                as in cards
                      or wits

                      or suicide.

August 15, 2017

Crying again because all those beautiful boys should have had the chance to get bored of each other. Instead, they lugged ashes to Washington, D.C. to throw at the White House lawn, to make meaning. To bury the dead of heart underneath the dead.

August 23, 2017

I just want to be the boy that gets taken home in pity.

I have forgotten gratitude.

October 22, 2017

James' favorite rocks: picture jasper, labradorite, hematite.

October 22, 2017

I am a good boy.

My body is sweet and sour.

November 26, 2017

Hi

December 14, 2017

My salvation. I make a snake from the clay and swallow him whole.

December 16, 2017

There has never been a more palpable moment than when I promised God loves you.

I meant it,

    but no one

        believed me.

April 16, 2018

Sometimes people spit on your body,

      and you don't get to fuck

your feelings away

           for a little while.

June 7, 2018

I made a family.

    Are you my family?

        Are we all family?

A family is much concerned

    with every

        broken

            bone.

June 19, 2018

I'm so disgusted with this protest I think about killing myself.

June 23, 2018

Some of my deeper wounds aren't pains but yearnings.

July 6, 2018

I'm tired of listening to poems about getting ghosted.

I'm tired of listening to poems about Tinder.

July 7, 2018

It's not impressive to a vegan that I can crack eggs with one hand.

July 8, 2018

She wants to see Jon Gosselin do a striptease for her birthday.

July 13, 2018

Joey from the Bike Stop

July 18, 2018

I am so bored.

Everyone is wearing cotton at this reading.

I thought she was falling in love with me.

August 1, 2018

a poem about this summer called "sex work at brunch"

August 21, 2018

make James a shirt that says *"venomous not poisonous"*

August 26, 2018

synonyms for leaving

September 26, 2018

Send later //

Hey, so I just wanted to reach out and see if you maybe wanted to try and sit down and talk some things out. It's been painful and sad to be so distant from you since our fight in August. If there's a means to salvage this friendship, I'd like to try. If not, I'd just like to know.

October 7, 2018

get Evan the Nana Grizol album on vinyl

October 26, 2018

I should have known it'd go out with a bang. I won't wait in the attic for her to come back.

Jan 3, 2019

use the word malingering in a poem

January 8, 2019

Write about that time you fled the smoking bar to avoid your sexual assaulter. You can't even hide in places that make you feel unwell.

January 21, 2019

It's the fucking year of abandonment.

January 26, 2019

What the fuck is a Roth IRA?

February 4, 2019

use queepling in a poem

February 6, 2019

fractious

February 8, 2019

Horatio, the fastest duck in the city.

February 20, 2019

I don't think I'll ever get over this, whatever the fuck this is.

February 23, 2019

Send later //

Hey, I wanted to reach out after giving this a fair amount of space. Losing you as a friend has been incredibly painful, to say the least.

Let me know what you think.

February 24, 2019

quaffable

May 8, 2019

A room full of loss. That friend who went away when you said you wouldn't support her abusive relationship anymore. That guy who whispered cartoon quotes to you in between sucking you off. All the friends who vanished. The death of love. The feeling that you'll never get back what you've lost. You are full of abandoned wishes.

May 31, 2019

aplomb

July 2, 2019

I see dead birds everywhere.

July 13, 2019

"You are now entering the Sourlands."

July 17, 2019

"Bird Songs of a Killjoy"

July 19, 2019

I've got bruises from all the people I let fuck me lately.

July 20, 2019

Write a poem called "whiskey dick."

July 21, 2019

Write a poem called "The Triumphant Return of the Cloud Billboard."

July 28, 2019

bad for me I know
but I stick frozen french fries
in the oven and forget
I busy myself reading old postcards
from people I don't talk to
organize my pocket knife collection
dust the piano, wait for him
to text me back to look for confirmation

I'm right to lean into his soft parts

August 1, 2019

Canadian pawn shops are amazing

August 10, 2019

Arrowwood Farms

August 12, 2019

Say a prayer for Ramon.

August 19, 2019

Do you think I'm lucky because I almost died when I was born?

August 29, 2019

He could drive the whole state of Colorado and not think of me. He could.

September 1, 2019

I wanna be that body that he worries about that he wants to protect that he wants to put gloves on for.

September 12, 2019

a reprise to honor and shame

September 25, 2019

get a tattoo of a peach

October 12, 2019

He tries to kiss you in the gas station in rural Maryland, and you panic. He doesn't get it. He doesn't know what it was like to be fed dirt by boys in pickup trucks.

October 15, 2019

Get James a citywide special T-Shirt.

November 4, 2019

When you ever have time, start a small press and name your small press Freetime Press.

November 5, 2019

Try to figure out the name of the cute queer who works at the Annenberg.

December 27, 2019

Write the poem as a novel? What parts do you keep? Do you skip J altogether? Sex, excess, trauma, quiet contemplation, love, relationship to yourself.

December 29, 2019

they put blackberries into your mouth
that pop like fish eggs, stain your teeth
they can throw you on the bed
and shove inside of you, make a fist
out of you and make a fist that you'll blow
your load into and you can hear
the whimper like it hurts to touch you
it hurts you to look at a boy so beautiful
in this tiny room where you're both panting
and dripping
and soft as rocks

January 5, 2020

Hitch in voice, magical, numinous. The day he said he could smell me on him and all the places I've smelled since then. See the queerness in sidecar motocross.

January 10, 2020

Wants. Grace.

January 31, 2020

E said you were beautiful, like Niagara Falls

February 3, 2020

You're allergic to cats.

February 4, 2020

a family of psychics eating dinner together in their psychic lounge

February 8, 2020

Buy James crappy taxidermy.

February 12, 2020

It's okay. It's like summer peaches. And June strawberries. Fruit has seasons.

February 20, 2020

Dr. Jared Liebman

February 23, 2020

Overheard: *"And basically, the rats just did nothing but cocaine until they died."*

February 26, 2020

Write a novel about the year of abandonment.

March 8, 2020

Only ten bucks to get laid in Texas feels worth it.

March 13, 2020

During the pandemic, when everything feels like sadness or disgust, this man still sees fit to wash his car's rims while his ass hangs fully out of his jeans.

March 14, 2020

In the dream you get way too drunk, you lie on the floor and James tells you they're going to Caitlin's. You don't remember this at 4 AM when you wake up half-naked and covered in beer on the dance floor and someone helps you get home. You're frantic about what happened to James and where they are. You call them for the thousandth time when they finally walk in and act like what happened was normal. You think seriously about breaking up with them on the spot, but some stray cats break into the house and interrupt you just as you wake up for real this time.

March 15, 2020

Go to Lucky's Last Chance with James when things are open.

March 22, 2020

10% of everyone is both bisexual and impossible.

March 23, 2020

The government doesn't want you to see your mom.

Do you want to?

March 31, 2020

For E's birthday, you will make all the cakes.

April 1, 2020

When the world stopped I jerked off. I sucked on my own nipples. I licked my computer screen hoping to taste the cumshot. When the world stopped I stuck a bottle up my ass, I drank the dregs of your beer, I humped the arm of the couch and hoped that would get me off in time to jump off the roof.

April 18, 2020

Is it time again to put my mouth on things? Please?

April 20, 2020

I couldn't stop writing about him if I wanted to. He is marvelous, and I want to say it in a million ways.

April 26, 2020

Languor, use it in a poem.

April 27, 2020

Fatness and who is fat and who is not, and what that means for your fat self.

May 12, 2020

26 inch thigh, 38 inch waist, 43 inch ass.

May 16, 2020

You hid E's birthday presents on the floor of your bedroom closet.

May 23, 2020

Feep, when you poke someone with your foot

May 24, 2020

Write a poem about the time you smoked weed with the male models, and then you got lost in the woods, and a stranger had to help you back to your tent in the dark. The models wouldn't stop saying your name in unison like an inside joke. You drank their Miller Lites embedded in the creek's rocks to keep them cool. Your ex-friend was camping with your group, and you couldn't bear to spend another minute there because it made you too sad. These male models on leave from New York City for the weekend were goofy, affable, and just the salve you needed. You thought you might kiss each and every one of them. Crossfaded from their generosity of booze and weed, you couldn't see your tent in the dark. You walked to the nearest fire and asked if they'd help you. A man took your arm in his and walked you a hundred yards in the opposite direction you'd been heading and put you to bed like a careful parent.

May 25, 2020

Buy that rubber jock harness for James.

June 9, 2020

I love you like a human being loves a human being.

July 20, 2020

Eating peaches feels like falling in love with him.

July 27, 2020

I'll suck them in like a shipwreck.

July 29, 2020

Write a poem called "2 cute 2 b forgotten" about how James hasn't thought about doing special things for you lately.

August 4, 2020

(To the tune of the hymn "What Wondrous Love is This?") *What fresh hell is this?*

August 5, 2020

The summer I lost myself. The summer
of abandon. When I fell in love
with withholding and repression,
with lunch time cum shots.
Making out in the corner
at the Hop Along show. A mouth
that I wanted, that was nothing, intangible pieces.
Don't worry, I turned out alright.
Later, in January, in the hot tub,
I finally let it go, let it out
in the basement at the karaoke party.
So that I can let it go,
so that I can cruise in a bookstore
and fall in love with the back of a head.

August 7, 2020

Name a cat Disco.

August 8, 2020

How do I feed myself outside of summer with its peaches and tomatoes?

August 24, 2020

Write a poem called "Pervert Land."

August 20, 2020

A bat swoops down and taps into the hat of this girl on your roof. She tells you she's been bitten by a bat twice

and each time it was while she was fucking her ex-girlfriend.

August 22, 2020

Fescue, lichen, quartz, the Hudson Valley. The valley of yearning.

August 23, 2020

Old, tired, torn, and curled like roadkill.

August 26, 2020

Write a love poem about Jerry Falwell Jr.'s love of cuckolding.

Call the poem "Junior."

August 30, 2020

A fetish dating app called Tustler.

August 31, 2020

Overheard: *"Being present is for roller coasters and cumming"*

September 13, 2020

moral injury

September 21, 2020

Overheard: *"I can't imagine anyone having sex with her. She's just so random."*

October 3, 2020

Buy something exciting for camping for E.

October 6, 2020

Buy James a good puzzle.

October 10, 2020

Make a Sugar Bottom Rail Club T-shirt.

Make a college-style sweatshirt that just says BOTTOM.

October 17, 2020

Buy E a poetry prompt book for Christmas.

October 19, 2020

I'm desperate for a dinner that's not coming.

October 24, 2020

App idea: a Google calendar to keep track of who you've hugged during the pandemic and when.

October 25, 2020

Camp Rough Velvet Valley

October 31, 2020

Write a book about the cowboys from the Gay Rodeo you love to go to each year.

November 11, 2020

Use the word libidinous.

November 12, 2020

Make a baking website where directions are given, like "While the cake bakes, give your boyfriend a blowjob."

November 14, 2020

Walked around and tried to find new love songs to remind me of you, but every song that came on was sadder than the last one.

November 24, 2020

Thinking about my body moving in this world, less weight on my chest. No more slumping over in front of the bathroom mirror to avoid looking at myself. I thank them for their time, but I am excited to be the body that lives underneath them.

November 25, 2020

"I'm Marie Kondoing my tits."

November 30, 2020

Earworms passed like a disease from lover to lover.

December 1, 2020

Ask E about the conversation you had at Ridley Creek State Park where you felt close to God.

December 18, 2020

Write about sex and self-injury, is there grace in fucking strangers even when it can hurt you? Write about the value of giving yourself over to cruising.

December 30, 2020

Write about having such little awareness of your chest at age 11 that your dad had to snag you by the collar of your shirt and tell you that you needed *to put on a fucking bra* before you ran over to the neighbor's house.

January 1, 2021

Write a country song called "Even Tough Guys Need to Get Fucked Softly Sometimes."

January 17, 2021

Write a country song called "Old Dog at the Wawa."

January 19, 2021

I love cruising because it offers me a chance to see how people perceive my gender without first having to establish a lot of intimacy. I get to say who I am, and then the guys who see me that way accept that. It's an individualistic sense of self that is controlled by my own hands.

February 12, 2021

use the word tinhorn

February 21, 2021

500,000 Covid deaths in your prayers for the people this week.

March 13, 2021

Write about how modern tools help you cruise as a trans person. Like when you get called to the Bike Stop basement by a Scruff message and you feel safe knowing that the guy knows who you are already. No surprises.

March 14, 2021

Name your bar Scout's Tearoom.

April 9, 2021

You bought E underwear for his birthday.

May 16, 2021

This week's prayers of the people: may we recognize each other.

May 31, 2021

Write about honeysuckles and bird watching with E.

June 2, 2021

You bought E those crew socks for their birthday, and they're in the drawer in your closet.

June 9, 2021

You buy yourself some dick for your birthday.

        You kick him out when he tries to snuggle you.

June 27, 2021

What are you waiting for?

July 1, 2021

And then there's most of a fist inside your asshole and you're vibrating with possibility. The possibility that you never knew what you needed, that what heals wounds and sparks bright in the crepuscular parts of your brain would come along when you weren't looking. You left your optimism at the door but

drank heavily from it first.

July 6, 2021

Cute guy at the Bike Stop is named Kyle.

July 14, 2021

"I am the autumn and the scarlet. I am the makeup on your eyes."

July 20, 2021

You used to bike up 18th Street and dream. You would bite yourself in your dreams. You would pierce yourself. What dreams did you deserve? That they wouldn't adopt the cat? Buy the house? Refinance the mortgage? What did you even want from them? You swallowed them. Became blood brothers. What is this waking up? What is this wanting more? You bike up 18th now and think about new love. You bike, and you want to cry a little because you're listening to The Breeders to prevent the hardening of your heart. You vibrate along with your fenders and your loose handlebars. You need a new story, but you keep telling yourself an old story. In the new story, you'll never get hurt, and you won't daydream.

July 21, 2021

The one who got away walks into the Bike Stop.

August 20, 2021

Call your dance party "Physical."

September 3, 2021

Write about a haunted house. Haunted by gender? Haunted by violence? The ghost of someone who never got to be himself.

September 12, 2021

Stay at the Bird's Nest Bed and Breakfast with E.

September 22, 2021

Overheard: *"All cock will be uncut cock in the apocalypse."*

October 2, 2021

Write a poem called "To See and Be Seen."

October 10, 2021

What beauty is there in an unjust world? What moves you? You are cleansed of your sins. You pray alone and drool a little against the stained glass. You prepare for surgery. You mistake excitement for nervousness. You tell the ex-Mormon that you're a good Christian boy. When you should be listening, you're drooling again instead, wondering if she thought you were less cute because of it.

October 17, 2021

Buy James a telescope.

November 12, 2021

The queer girl who died by suicide from your hometown this week was named Eliza.

December 25, 2021

Robins murmuring at dusk on Christmas. Like summer.

When anything is possible

and everything smells like sweat.

                                          Your whole body aches with want.

January 18, 2022

I have four chin hairs.

January 23, 2022

Free lemon Jell-O shots. Nothing is as vibrant as it once was.

January 24, 2022

Write about your ancestors. The legacy of masculinity. Write about German foods. Write about stories your Dad told you as a kid. The stolen car, the bookies,

the secretly queer friend who died alone.

January 27, 2022

After several weeks of testosterone, I've started dreaming of my physical transition. I wake from dreams where I've always had a mustache, and I transform my belly into a hard barrel.

January 28, 2022

My Great-Grandfather, George Washington Keck Bernstiel (what a name!) is the originator of Dad's dumpling soup and slow-cooked beef and hand-cut noodle stew.

February 17, 2022

Alone at the Bike Stop, the handsome man talks to you with charisma and kindness. It's fifteen minutes before he says, *"well, you're a lesbian or something, right? You understand,"* and your wings feel clipped.

February 20, 2022

You try to reframe panic attacks as your body being full of its functions.

Piss and blood,

                                                                    piss and blood.

February 24, 2022

Buy James a new snake shirt for their birthday.

February 25, 2022

"Now we've got Bear Blood" to the tune of Taylor Swift's "Bad Blood"

March 15, 2022

90 days on testosterone, and you've got so much blood.

March 23, 2022

You're moody, you're sad, you're untenable. You're high, you're alone. You're full of it. You're chasing something.

You are scared to have built your life around others. So move out.

March 24, 2022

I need too much. I am too much.

March 25, 2022

I don't want to talk. I want to listen to "Running Up That Hill" covers.

March 30, 2022

How can we expand on those times you trust me
you feel like you're standing on solid ground
even when something threatening comes along?

March 31, 2022

Testosterone makes me feel like if I don't come several times a day, I might die. I now plan my orgasms around meetings and interruptions, around boyfriends coming over to the house who I think might not want to have sex on my schedule. It's like I am secreting away my hard-ons.

April 2, 2022

Buy a mustache comb for E.

April 3, 2022

Tell E about the Baltimore dream.

April 4, 2022

Make noodle soup for E on top surgery day.

April 11, 2022

Write about learning to feel pleasure from novelty.

April 26, 2022

Some kind of perfect symmetry to get cummed on by that guy on his boat on a spring day when I'm feeling floaty and warm and free and desperately in love with E. Just like that brisk night back in 2019 when I popped a half-pint in my pocket and texted E to tell him he was everything to me. He's since seen the roller coaster of me. I walk by a dyke couple and think *that's me*, and then I let the boat guy cum on me and think, *that's me*. E makes a slut joke about me, and I tell him to be good, and we make plans to move to a lake house, and we make plans to hang out with my Brooklyn hookup, and I tell him I would marry him if I believed in marriage and I take care of him when he can't move his arms, and he takes care of me when I can't sleep again. And I think, what love, what good luck.

May 4, 2022

Felix Gonzalez Torres

"Untitled" (Water)

May 21, 2022

Summer sucks me in like a flooded river. It's the season I fall in and out of love with myself. It's the train ride to New York, feeding him energy bars, staring out the window, and crying to old songs. I cross the Delaware and see the Trenton Makes sign like that morning ten years ago when I was finally free from you. The Japanese knot wood, the poison ivy, and the wild wheat have sprung green overnight. Yesterday, there were nuggets of hail hitting me on the head, and today it's summer! I took so many trips to New York this year to be alone and think about who would ever understand me. The project that lasts forever. Each trip to New York is more expensive than the last, but who counts money when there's independence and sweat to be had? Sex parties and bodega sandwiches. Sleepless and always catching up. Sand in my shoes from the Rockaways. Another quick nap on the train by the water.

> Summer takes, and takes, and takes.

May 22, 2022

I wanna go home with him. I wanna watch him kiss other boys. I wanna lay in the grass and suck him off. I wanna stay out til 3 AM at the fuck party in Chinatown.

June 1, 2022

Pup.

June 12, 2022

Name your dance party "Glue."

June 27, 2022

Ten years since you laid on the floor of your apartment and contemplated freedom, just as Katie Holmes filed for divorce from Tom Cruise. You bought cigarettes again. You got on the train that night to Philadelphia and hid out for weeks. You cried until you were too sore to eat. You felt light for the first time in your life.

June 29, 2022

I'm afraid all these fears are true.

June 30, 2022

Make art that asks hard questions.

    Paradoxical questions.

Let them grow from the truest place.

    Nothing pat or theraperized.

July 11, 2022

Sing "My Own Worst Enemy" at Karaoke tomorrow.

July 18, 2022

Write a poem about the Schmidt sting pain scale.

July 25, 2022

How do you write about a lifetime of disappointment?

August 13, 2022

We find our path the old way, with novel landmarks: the rusted-out car dumped in the woods, the dried-out piece of honeycomb, and the dog tied up that won't quiet.

August 20, 2022

buy James a golden kazoo for Christmas

August 23, 2022

A man in Brooklyn says *lucky me*
before he sticks his cock in

August 25, 2022

that's why so easy to smoke
that's why so easy to drink
to sniff poppers
to fuck strangers

August 28, 2022

I couldn't believe the things I had missed out on with you
the year that followed I moved forward and then backward
talking to beautiful new people
returning to the crater of my life again—
to rummage through old emails
to wonder when you'd return home.
Then, to be alive again.

August 31, 2022

What is there for me? Let's find out.

Boston Gordon (he/they) is a poet from Philadelphia, Pennsylvania. He is the author of the chapbook *Glory Holes* (Harbor Editions, 2022). He runs the award-winning *You Can't Kill A Poet* reading series—which highlights queer and trans identified writers in Philadelphia. He has poems published in many places like *Guernica*, *American Poetry Review*, and *Best New Poets*.

About Small Harbor Publishing

Small Harbor Publishing is a 501c3 nonprofit organization. Our goal is to publish unique and diverse voices. We are a feminist press, and we are committed to diversity and inclusion. We strive to bring new voices to a devoted and expanding readership.

Small Harbor Publishing began in 2018 with the first issue of *Harbor Review*. The magazine is an online space where poetry and art converse. *Harbor Review* quickly grew and now publishes reviews and runs multiple micro chapbook competitions, including the Washburn Prize and the Editor's Prize.

In July 2020, Small Harbor Publishing was officially incorporated and began Harbor Editions. Harbor Editions accepts submissions through a chapbook open reading period, a hybrid chapbook open reading period, the Marginalia Series, and the Laureate Prize.

In 2023, Harbor Anthologies began with a mission to promote texts that explore social justice issues and highlight marginalized writers.

If you would like to support Small Harbor Publishing, please visit our "About" page at smallharborpublishing.com/about.

www.ingramcontent.com/pod-product-compliance
Lightning Source LLC
LaVergne TN
LVHW092051060526
838201LV00047B/1335